To Judy-
Woof!
Debra Ekm
Dakota, Zoe, Am
Patch, Tom, Scout,
Zip + Jake

The DOG BOOK

WHAT YOU SHOULD KNOW ABOUT DOGS

Debra Ekman

HILLIARD HARRIS

HILLIARD HARRIS

P.O. Box 275
Boonsboro, Maryland 21713-0275

The Dog Book, What You Should Know About Dogs

First Edition-September 2006
ISBN 1-59133-183-8

Manufactured/Printed in the United States of America
2006

TABLE OF CONTENTS

Sales of this book benefit Your Dog's Friend, a free service to advise and educate dog owners before they choose their dog, after they bring home their new pet, and when they have concerns about their dog's behavior. For more information about Your Dog's Friend, check our website, www.yourdogsfriend.info.

ACKNOWLEDGEMENTS

For this booklet, the following websites and books were particularly helpful:

www.petsforlife.org
www.gooddogz.org
www.MarylandSPCA.org

✱*Mutts: America's Dogs* by Brian Kilcommons and Michael Capuzzo

✱*Choosing and Caring for a Shelter Dog* by Bob Christiansen

✱*Adopt the Perfect Dog* by Gwen Bailey

✱*Paws to Consider* by Brian Kilcommons and Sarah Wilson

✱the Animal Behavior College curriculum.

I also appreciate the advice of Ann Roseberry Lincoln, a trainer in the Washington, DC area, as well as the editing and layout of Shawn and Stephanie Reilly.

INTRODUCTION

I love dogs! I love watching them play and lounge in the sun. I love hearing their deep sighs of contentment. I love how they huddle together and how, five minutes after they quarrel, one will lay his head on the other's back. I love the simplicity of their lives. Sometimes, I even envy it.

Of course, I get to see all this because my dogs have the shelter, food, love and attention that all dogs need. There are too many that don't. There are too many dogs in shelters, and there are too many dogs euthanized every year. Yet, dogs aren't born aggressive, and they are social animals.

I think the problem is that most dog owners don't understand what their dog needs or how their dog learns. First, they choose the wrong dog for their lifestyle. Then, they provide basic care and wait for their dog to become the perfect family pet. Sometimes, it works out. Too often, it doesn't. When they face issues they never expected, even well-meaning owners can become stressed and overwhelmed.

I have ten adopted dogs. You would think that, somewhere along the line, I would have figured out all that I needed to know. But until I decided to study dog behavior and training, I didn't understand what motivates dogs or how they think. Until I volunteered at a rescue and shelters, I didn't recognize that dog owners give up their dogs because of problems that could have been prevented in the first place.

I do have some biases you should know about. I wish more people would get their dogs from shelters and rescues, and I wish more people would realize the benefits of adult dogs over puppies. But no matter where you found your dog or what kind of dog he is, this booklet will help you better understand your pet and his needs. **Please read every section**, even if one doesn't seem relevant to you. You'll find information helpful to all dog owners throughout.

You will find some instances where I suggest using treats as rewards. One of the complaints I hear is that dog owners can't have treats on them all the time. In the beginning, carry a treat pouch, have treats stashed around the house, or put treats in your pocket. You will be able to phase out the treats over time. They are only a training tool. It is worth meeting with a dog trainer or taking an obedience class to help you use this tool. Both you and your dog will be better off for it.

Make sure you also check some of the books and websites listed in the back. If you are adopting a dog from a shelter or rescue, you will find two books particularly helpful: "Choosing and Caring for a Shelter Dog" by Bob Christiansen and "Adopt the Perfect Dog" by Gwen Bailey. There are also some short, easy-to-read booklets that lay out programs for dealing with specific dog behavior issues. Two websites, www.petsforlife.org and www.gooddogz.org, have tip sheets on a variety of dog-related topics; and you can find a resource library of articles at www.petfinder.com.

You can reach me and find more information at my website, www.yourdogsfriend.info. Together, we can help your dog become your lifetime companion.

1

THE SCOOP ON SHELTER AND RESCUE DOGS

I am partial to shelter and rescue dogs. Maybe it's because too many dogs end up in shelters through no fault of their own. There was a divorce; the owner is moving; the dog wasn't trained. Maybe it's because all of my dogs, ten at the moment, have been from shelters and rescues. All but one are mutts. I don't know how they started their lives or how they came to be throwaways, but I do know that they are now living their lives as devoted, loving family pets.

Shelters care for purebreds and mutts, strays and owner give-ups. Some rescues also take in all kinds of dogs, but many rescues are devoted to a particular breed.

Rescues generally place dogs in foster homes. Most shelters have onsite kennels and foster homes to house their dogs. So, if you don't see what you're looking for at a shelter, ask what other dogs they have in foster care. Also, check to see if a temperament evaluation has been done or request one after you apply for the dog.

It can be difficult to walk through a shelter because the dogs are usually under stress. Some bark for attention; some pine for their owners; some fight with their neighbors; while others curl up, as if to wish it all away. Children in particular can find visiting a shelter disconcerting. But I guarantee that you can find your dog in a shelter. Try squatting down sideways in front of the kennel and speak gently to the dog. See if the dog watches you quietly or comes over to greet you. Both are good responses. If you're choosing a puppy, look for the one that responds to you without throwing himself at you, and that seems able to calm down after a noise or sudden movement. On your visit outside the kennel, don't hover

over the dog, make direct eye contact, or reach over the dog's head. You want to help the dog stay calm.

Some dogs from shelters will be fearful at first, but you can help you dog overcome his fears in a number of ways.

✱Stick to a routine, even on weekends, so that he knows what to expect. His feeding, his walks, and his bedtime should be fairly consistent for the first few months.

✱Give your dog a safe place to escape, like in his crate or under a table. When you're home, leave the door to the crate open with toys and a few treats inside.

✱Help your dog gain confidence by teaching him some basic obedience. His training sessions should be short and FUN! Use positive reinforcement; punishment will only cause more stress.

✱Try hand feeding your dog to gain his trust. If your dog tends to hide, put small amounts of food around the house, so he is motivated to come out and is rewarded for his efforts.

✱If your dog is "hand shy", practice slowly raising your hand over his head, a little at a time, while giving him treats with your other hand.

✱Stay calm, so you don't reinforce his fears.

✱Try to desensitize your dog to what he's afraid of by slowly exposing him to the situation a little at a time. For example, if your dog is afraid of the veterinarian's office, take him to the office and leave again, without even seeing the vet. Give him treats to help him associate the trip with good things.

✱Get your dog out among strangers and other dogs, but never force him. If your dog is anxious, keep him at a distance, while you play with him or give him a treat. You may be able to gradually decrease the distance if your dog starts focusing on you, instead of his fears.

To prevent accidents and destructive behavior, you should leave your dog in a crate or confined area when you're not home. If you train your dog to the crate and put a dog bed and chew toys inside, he will see it as a safe, comforting den. Expose your dog to the crate slowly, making it a positive place by offering treats and meals there with the door open. Eventually, you can close the door, but increase the time gradually. Consider hiring a neighbor or dog walker to walk your dog during the day, so he isn't confined for more than four consecutive hours.

Remember that a bored dog is more likely to get into trouble. Your dog needs regular exercise, like long walks or runs or play dates with other active dogs. If your dog is too strong for you, buy a head collar, such as a Gentle Leader or Halti, or a no-pull harness, something like the Premier Easy Walk Harness, until you train him to walk without pulling. To keep your dog occupied when you're not home, give your dog what I call puzzle toys. You put treats in these toys, and your dog has to move the toy around to get the treats out. These include, among others, the Buster Cube, Tube and Groove, Molecule Ball, and Twist and Treat.

Sometimes, a dog is so stressed when his owner leaves that he barks, chews, scratches, or hurts himself. Some tips on helping your dog get over separation anxiety include:

✱Confine your dog to a crate when you go out. This den-like space will help your dog feel more secure while you're gone. Make sure you leave him with toys in his crate.

✱Don't always leave the house after confining him. Practice leaving for just a few minutes, so he will see that you always return. Keep your departures and arrivals calm.

✱Exercise your dog, especially in the mornings, and do a few minutes of obedience training to build his confidence.

✱When you leave, place a shirt with your scent in his crate and turn on a radio. You could also try Comfort Zone, a DAP (dog appeasing pheromone) diffuser, which releases an odor like that of a nursing mother dog, or Rescue Remedy, which is a mixture of plant essences that seem to have a calming effect.

✱Consider leaving your dog at doggie day care.

✱Don't punish your dog when you come home for whatever he did while you were gone.

✱In severe cases, talk to your vet about medication to help reduce your dog's anxiety.

I don't recommend most electronic training devices, including electronic collars, shock mats, or shriek alarms. I also stay away from training collars (sometimes called choke or slip collars) and prong collars. You are trying to build trust with a dog that has already been stressed, and there are positive, reward-based training alternatives. You should never startle a puppy under four months old or a shy dog, and you don't want to provoke an aggressive response from more dominant dogs.

Unless pit bulls are outlawed in your area, you will undoubtedly see a number of them at the shelter. So, let me address this issue. Unless the dog has been purposely neglected or abused, pit bulls can be good family pets.

They love people and are very affectionate and playful. However, like any dog, they should not be left alone with young children. And if you have more than one dog, the pit should be kept separate when no one is home, even if the dogs are best friends. After puppyhood, a pit should not be taken to dog parks. Dogs can look at each other the wrong way, and a fight can ensue. This can happen with all dogs, but pit bulls have strong jaws and they sometimes won't let go of another dog. If you want to know more about adopting pit bulls or other bully breeds, consult **Training Secrets for Bully Breeds**, available from **www.populardogs.com**. The articles in this magazine were written by pit bull owners and lovers, who give reasonable advice from their own experience.

Some people are afraid to adopt their dog from a shelter or rescue. Don't be. Give them time to adjust to their new surroundings. Remember that, like any other dog, they need love and consistency to thrive. These dogs are some of the most loyal companions you will ever find, and you will be lucky to have one in your life.

TEACHING YOUR DOG TO SIT

To teach your dog to sit, hold a treat at nose level and slowly move it over his head. As your dog looks up to follow the treat, his butt will start to go down. Say "GOOD" or use a clicker, as his butt hits the ground, and give him the treat. The motion of your hand upward is teaching your dog the hand signal for "SIT."

When you're sure your dog knows what you want, add the verbal cue, but do so just as your dog sits, so he doesn't have the opportunity to ignore your verbal request. Be careful not to repeat the cue. Saying "SIT, SIT, SIT" teaches your dog that the cue is "SIT, SIT, SIT." That's why he doesn't respond the **first** time you ask.

As the task becomes more difficult, the reward must be better. Although your dog may sit for kibble inside, you may need hot dog pieces to teach him to sit outside with squirrels running around.

2

WHAT YOU SHOULD KNOW BEFORE ADOPTING A PUPPY

Let's start with the idea that puppies aren't for everyone, and that may include you. Puppies are playful, developing dogs that chew, nip, jump, and have accidents. They need to be housebroken, supervised, exercised, socialized, and trained. Puppies younger than six months old need to be fed three or four times a day. A puppy's medical needs include vaccinations at six to eight weeks, with two sets of follow-up vaccines three to four weeks apart. Puppies also need to be spayed or neutered. Some vets will do the surgery as early as eight weeks, but it should definitely be done before six months, when most dogs reach sexual maturity.

Housebreaking requires routine and constant supervision. Puppies need to go out after they eat, sleep, drink, play, and before bed. When you are first housebreaking a puppy, it's a good idea to take him out every two hours. If you get in the habit of saying something like "go to the bathroom" just before you can see your puppy going, you can teach him to go on cue. You can train your dog to go in a particular area by consistently taking him there. If you can place his feces where you want him to go, the smell will also encourage him. Going to the bathroom and going for a walk should be different issues. Otherwise, you will be forced to go for a walk to get your puppy to eliminate, even if you're sick or there's a blizzard.

When you take your puppy out, give him an extra ten minutes after he goes to make sure he has emptied his bladder fully. Inside, closely supervise your puppy. Keep him with you, either putting him in an X-pen, which is like a puppy playpen, or leaving his leash on. If you see him start to go inside, interrupt him, get him outside quickly, and praise him for going. If you're too late, don't punish him. If you do, he may learn to be afraid to go to the bathroom in your presence. Take him outside to remind him where to go, and clean the accident inside with an enzymatic cleaner, like Nature's Miracle, to remove the scent.

When you can't supervise him, your puppy should be in a crate. On average, puppies can only hold their urine for an hour longer than their age in months. In other words, you can't leave your three-month old puppy for longer than four hours. Although some dog owners hate the idea of using a crate, your puppy will see it as a comforting den, as long as you take the time to train him to the crate and leave toys for him. Your dog's crate should **not** be in a basement away from family activities. It's probably a good idea to have two crates—one where your family tends to gather and another in the bedroom, so your dog can be near you when you sleep.

Crates can only be effective for housebreaking if you use the right size. Some crates have an insert, so the crate can be enlarged as the puppy grows. Otherwise, put a box in the back to take up space. Your dog should not be able to go to the bathroom at one end, and then comfortably lie down at the other. As a rule of thumb, the crate should be one and a half times the length of your dog, without his tail, so he has room to stand up and turn around. Don't leave absorbent materials, like towels, in the crate. Otherwise, your pup will pee on the towel and kick it out of his way. This will greatly slow housebreaking.

Puppies teethe until about six months of age and continue to chew much longer. They also explore with their mouths. Your dog's food should be hard without a lot of grains and fillers. Have a frozen washcloth available for teething, and rotate your puppy's toys so they always seem new and interesting. Unless your puppy is confined when left alone, expect him to chew whatever is available. That includes furniture, carpet, walls, and clothes.

When you buy chew toys, stay away from toys that resemble your children's toys, your shoes, or the fringes of your rugs. Some of the better chew toys are Nylabones, Kongs, sterilized bones, and Galileo bones. To make them even more appealing, soak Nylabones in beef or chicken broth for fifteen minutes, and stuff the hole in Kongs or sterilized bones with cheese or peanut butter. The Galileo bones are expensive, but are good for strong chewers and can last for years. For a dog bed, consider the Toughchew Dog's Nest, carried by Orvis for Dogs. If your dog is able to chew through the bed's material, you get your money back.

Nipping and rough play are natural to puppies. However, wrestling with your puppy, playing tug of war, or roughhousing are never good ideas:

*Your puppy will get over-stimulated and mouth more.

*Your puppy will learn that aggressive behavior is tolerated.

*Your puppy will be practicing dominance over his pack leader.

Loudly exclaim, "OUCH", as if you've been hurt, when your puppy nips. Then, give your puppy an appropriate chew toy, and reward his calm behavior. If your puppy jumps on you, turn your back and wait. When he has all four feet on the ground, turn back, praise him, and give him a treat. If your puppy can't calm down, you want to remove your attention by walking out of the room. To get the dog you want, you have to teach your puppy appropriate behavior.

Your puppy also needs to be socialized to help him avoid becoming a fearful or aggressive dog. Before four months of age, you should expose your puppy to as many new situations as possible. He should meet all kinds of people—children, teenagers, adult men and women; go to the park, shopping centers, busy streets, and soccer games; allow you to touch his whole body and remove his food and toys; interact with cats and other dogs. Even though your puppy won't be fully vaccinated until about five months old, let your puppy meet friends' dogs if you know they are healthy and up to date on vaccines. After your puppy's second vaccination, generally between ten and sixteen weeks of age, you should enroll him in a puppy class to further socialize him to other dogs and strangers. If your puppy is frightened in class, go at his pace. Redirect his attention to a food treat or toy and encourage him gently.

If you're unsure if a puppy is right for you, let's tackle some myths about adult dogs. Contrary to popular belief, **adult dogs can be trained**. They have, in fact, been adopted and trained by law enforcement and service organizations. Adult dogs can bond to you and become devoted, loyal companions. Adult dogs can be less trouble than puppies. They are calmer, better able to hold their bladder, and less likely to chew. And when you adopt an adult dog, you know what you're getting. You will see changes in his personality as he becomes more comfortable in his new home, but his size and temperament are already formed.

One more thing: Whether you adopt a puppy or an adult dog, make sure you think through what type of dog fits your lifestyle. This doesn't mean that you only research and consider purebreds. In fact, mutts sometimes have fewer temperament issues than some of the most popular and over-bred breeds. What it does mean, though, is that you don't pick a Border Collie mix if you are a couch potato or a Weimaraner if this is your first dog. Don't go for the adorable puppy that will grow bigger than you can handle or the cute, small dog whose constant barking will drive you crazy. Don't pick the toy dog that is too fragile for the rough and tumble play of your children. Let others, with different priorities and needs, adopt them. Choose a dog that you can love forever, train him to be your well-behaved companion, and ENJOY!

Dogs need:

- Socialization
- Leadership
- Training
- Consistency
- Attention
- Exercise
- Mental Stimulation
- Appropriate Toys
- Quality, hard food

Dogs don't need:

- Punishment

3
YOUR DOG'S POINT OF VIEW

You will be able to train your dog and solve most problems if you understand some basic truths about dogs.

Dogs learn by association. If you put treats between your dog's paws when he goes "DOWN," your dog will learn to like the "down" position. If you let your dog nibble treats from your hand when he walks next to you, he will want to walk next to you. You will be able to phase out the treats, but the association will remain. Similarly, if you call your dog to give him a bath or to punish him, your dog will learn not to come. He will associate coming to you with something bad happening.

Force is never a good idea. I don't recommend training (sometimes called choke or slip) collars or prong collars (that pinch the dog's skin), even for training. They are never appropriate for young or timid dogs, and they can make an aggressive dog's behavior worse. Punishing your dog is also a bad idea. Your dog may learn to be afraid of you. He may not know why he is being punished or what you want. You may have unintended consequences when your dog forms a negative association with a desired behavior. For example, if you punish your dog for peeing in the house, you have taught him not to pee in front of you.

Dogs repeat behaviors that get them what they want. Your dog wants food, toys, playtime, walks, and attention. Your dog naturally chews, jumps, barks, urinates, and defends himself when he feels threatened. Imagine you're in a foreign country, and you don't understand the language or culture. That's your dog's world! He has to figure out what to do to get what he wants. So, help him by rewarding him for obeying training commands or exercising good manners. And when he does something that may be natural to him, but inappropriate to you, teach him an alternative that will be rewarded. He can urinate outside, not inside, and he can chew on the chew toy, not the furniture. The easiest reward is food, but dogs with a strong prey drive may prefer playing with a ball. Remember that your dog, like any foreigner, has to constantly interpret, so practice with him and be consistent.

Dogs were bred for a purpose. Herding dogs herd. Guarding dogs guard. Terriers dig. So, when your herding dog nips at your children's heels, he isn't being aggressive. Your herding dog needs training and **lots of exercise**. When your gentle dog, bred to guard his people and possessions, barks aggressively at the neighborhood children running around your house, he isn't acting out of character. Separate him from the children and appreciate that he is a good protector of your family. And that terrier that you thought was so cute may not seem so cute now that he's digging holes in your yard. But his job was to dig for gophers or rats or other vermin. Instead of getting frustrated with him for doing what he was bred to do, teach him to dig in a particular area by hiding toys and treats there. Fill holes he has made elsewhere with chicken wire, dog feces, or rocks and then cover them with soil.

Dogs need a leader to stabilize their world. You need to let your dog know that you are in charge, not by punishing or bullying your dog, but by using signals that your dog will understand. When you walk your dog, ask him to wait until you go out the door first, and train him to walk beside you unless you give him permission to explore. Tell your dog to "SIT" before you feed him, put on his leash, or play with him. Learn to ignore your dog's pushy behavior. Don't pet your dog when he nudges your hand. Don't feed your dog when he barks for food. Turn away from your dog when he jumps on you. Whether your dog is dominant or submissive, a dog that knows that you are the leader will feel more secure and behave better.

Dogs are social animals. Your dog will chew, bark, jump, or grab something and run if that's the only way to get your attention. If your dog takes something, don't chase him, or it will be a rewarding game. Instead, trade him for one of his toys. If your dog jumps on you, turn away. When he stops, turn back and ask him to sit. Then, praise and reward him. Your dog will quickly understand that jumping doesn't get your attention; sitting does. You should get in the habit of petting and praising your dog when he is lying quietly next to you. Reward good behavior, not just in training, but all the time.

If you are willing to see the world through your dog's eyes, you can teach your dog a great deal. Try to understand how he develops, how he learns, and what he needs. In return, he will give you back undying love and companionship.

Teach your dog basic obedience commands.

Training tends to establish the proper relationship between dog and owner, increase a dog's confidence, help him control his impulses, and provide alternatives to problem behaviors.

4
DOGS AND CHILDREN

A dog can be a wonderful companion for a child, but you have to be willing to work at the relationship. If you want a safe, peaceful household, you need to train your dog and set limits on your child. Unless you are a dog person who can't imagine living without a dog, it's probably best to wait until your child is five or six years old before getting a dog. At this age, your child should be able to understand the rules and have good motor control. Meanwhile, you can teach your child about dogs by showing him how to approach friends' and neighbors' dogs.

When meeting a dog, your child should ask the owner if it's okay to pet the dog. He should never approach a dog that is alone, tied up, in a car, or behind a fence. Even a nice dog can become territorial if he feels threatened. If the owner gives permission, your child should first put his hand out, palm down, to let the dog smell his scent. He should not pet the dog on his head, but under his chin or on his chest. Teach your child not to look the dog directly in the eye, not to hug the dog, not to scream, and not to run around the dog. You are teaching your child to be safe by being gentle and respectful.

When you are ready to get a dog, keep in mind that you, and not your child, should make the decision. Don't pick a dog because your daughter thinks he's cute or your son thinks he's tough looking. You have to consider the dog's size and temperament, your willingness to work with the dog, and the activity level in your household. Don't get a dog to teach your child responsibility. No matter how your child pleads and promises, other activities will come up, he'll get bored, or leave home for camp or college. You, the adult, has to want the dog and be willing to take care of him.

Especially when children are involved, choose your dog carefully. And never leave young children unsupervised around your dog.

✱Toy breeds are very delicate and can be hurt when a child hugs them too hard, picks them up incorrectly, or drops them.

✱Small dogs can be easily provoked to bite if they feel cornered. So, teach your child not to follow a dog if he moves away; the dog is signaling that he wants to be alone.

✱Herding dogs may nip at a child's heels or backside. If you want a herding dog, your children should be older or less rambunctious.

✱Large dogs can scratch or knock over a child without meaning any harm. Consider the size and strength of your children and your willingness to put time into training.

✱Dogs bred as guardians can act aggressively toward visiting children when they cause too much commotion. They may not be a good choice if you have a lot of your children's friends over.

When you bring home your new dog, let him explore your yard first. He will feel more relaxed outside and will have a chance to go to the bathroom. Although your children will be excited to see the dog, ask them to wait inside. When you bring your dog in, give them each a treat for your dog, but have them wait until the dog comes to them. Show them how to give the dog a treat with their palm up and how to pet the dog's chest or chin. Dogs can have sensitive necks; so, warn them not to hug your dog for at least the first few weeks, until you decide the dog trusts them. Remind them not to squeal or chase your dog, and give your children a new toy or game to help to give the dog a break. A shelter or rescue dog, in particular, needs time to adjust to his surroundings and needs for his experiences with children to be gradual and positive.

There are certain rules that your children must agree to if your family adopts a dog. They should never tease, pull the tail, ride, or run around your dog. Children should leave him alone if he's sleeping, eating, or chewing on a toy. A more difficult rule for some children is that they shouldn't chase your dog, roughhouse, wrestle, or play tug of war. These are games that your dog can win, especially as he gets older, making him feel dominant. When kids play in this way, they also can over-stimulate your dog and incite him to jump or nip. Smaller children may become scared, while older children are sometimes teaching your dog behaviors that are unacceptable. What your child can do is throw a ball or play fetch. It's also a good idea to teach your older children basic obedience commands and then enlist them to help with your dog's training.

If you already have a dog and are expecting a baby, plan ahead. Get your dog used to a baby's cry, the stroller, and the scent of baby powder. There is a CD, available from www.preparingfido.com that has recorded infant sounds, as well as written advice from the Humane Society of the US, on how to introduce your pet to your baby. Encourage friends with babies to visit and let your dog see you hold their baby. When you are in the hospital, send a blanket with your baby's scent home for your dog.

Once you and your baby are home, let your dog spend time with you both, and give your dog attention and treats in the baby's presence. This will help your dog develop a positive association with your baby. When visitors come over to see the baby, don't isolate your dog. Use a baby gate, rather than a closed door, when you need to keep your dog out of your baby's room.

Dogs can add so much to a family! In fact, some of your children's fondest memories will be time spent with the family pet. As the parent, however, you have the responsibility to teach both your children and your dog appropriate behavior.

5
MULTIPLE PETS

Most people I know with two dogs would never go back to having just one. Two pets can keep each other company and usually get more exercise. It's fun to watch two pets play and cuddle together. Some of us have kept going until we are the "proud parents" of three, five, or, like me, ten dogs. Keeping the peace among your dogs, much like among your children, is a balancing act. It can be made much easier, though, if you're careful about which dogs you choose, how you introduce them, and what your rules are for living together.

For two dogs, your best choice is usually a neutered male and a spayed female. Intact dogs can be more aggressive, and two dogs of the same sex are more likely to be quarrelsome. If you are considering a shelter dog, you can usually bring your resident dog to visit. Although the visit may be through a fence, you can tell if the dogs snarl, stare each other down, or become hyperactive. None of these are good signs. Ideally, the dogs should calmly assess each other.

When your new dog is ready to come home, prepare your resident dog by giving him a cloth with the new dog's scent. Have your dogs meet outside in an area that is unfamiliar to both of them, not at the house or in the park where you walk your dog every day. Ask a relative or friend to help you. Go for a walk with the dogs walking parallel, but loosely leashed. Let them gradually interact and sniff each other. Praise and treat their positive interactions. If one or both dogs start acting aggressively, calmly separate them and divert their attention. After a few minutes, try again.

Once your dogs have had time to adjust to each other, you can bring them home. Go outside with them before bringing them in, and keep their leashes on in case you have to restrain them. Use praise and treats when they behave. If one dog snarls or growls, separate them, distract them, and re-introduce them more slowly. If you have more than one dog at home, let them each meet your new dog separately, so they don't gang up on and scare him.

Remember that dogs establish their own pecking order and that there probably will be spats as they work out their issues with each other. In the beginning, your resident dog will be top dog, and you should reinforce this by giving him food, toys, and attention first. If it becomes obvious, after a period of time, that your new dog is more dominant, you should reverse the order. When your dogs are getting to know each other, don't panic if they fight and don't think that you will have to return or re-home the new dog. I once had two male dogs that had serious fights twice in their lives; for the ten years in between, they got along fine. Recognize that your more submissive dog(s) may feel anxious at times and want to be alone. Leave a crate open for that purpose.

When you have more than one dog, routine becomes critical. Feed your dogs in the same order and location every day. My dogs wait while I put down the other dogs' bowls because they know when it's their turn and where I will place their bowl. Without routine, your dogs won't know what to expect, and are likely to quarrel more often. Your dogs will also learn phrases when you repeat them consistently. When I say, "come on, guys, let's eat," they know exactly where to go. Remind your dogs that you are the leader. Every time you do something for them, ask them to do something for you first. For example, tell them to "SIT" before you put down their food bowls.

When you are thinking about adding a dog to your cat household, see if you can find out the dog's history with cats. Most shelters have this information for owner surrenders, and a few shelters will test their dogs with cats. If not, it may be helpful to see how the dog reacts if you quickly move a furry toy that squeaks. Some dogs try to "kill" squeaky toys, which may not be a good sign.

Cats will usually be afraid of dogs at first. Some will hide, while others will scratch at the dog to keep him away. So it's a good idea to separate the two with a door between them before they meet. Let them each smell the other's scent on your clothes and hands. Then, by rubbing both animals with the same cloth, you can give them similar scents. When they do meet, have your dog on a leash and your cat able to reach a high, safe place, like a bookcase. If the dog starts to chase the cat, say "NO" and hold on to his leash. Reward him for coming back to your side. You may also want to put up some baby gates, so your cat can get away without the dog following. It may take a few weeks for your cat to get used to your new dog, but many cats and dogs become fast friends.

Having two or more pets is not for everyone. It takes patience, consistency, and realistic expectations. Most of us who have more than one pet, though, wouldn't have it any other way!

6
TIPS FOR A NEW DOG:

✱Before your new dog comes home, make sure that everyone in your family agrees on the house rules, such as whether the dog will be allowed on the sofa and what rooms he will be allowed in. You also need to be sure that everyone uses the same words for behaviors that you are requesting. For example, "DOWN" may mean, "lie down " to you, and "get off the sofa" to your husband.

✱Get what you need immediately for your dog ahead of time. This should include a collar or halter; leash; identification tag; food bowl; water bowl; toys and chew toys; high quality food with protein, not filler; some of the food your dog is used to; baggies for picking up feces; an enzymatic cleaner, like Nature's Miracle; dog bed.

✱Try to pick up your dog at a time when he will have a day with you. However, don't stay home for a week if that's not your normal schedule. Your dog will have more trouble adjusting to your routine if he isn't exposed to it.

✱When you bring your dog home, let him first explore your yard. He will feel more relaxed and will have a chance to go to the bathroom. When he goes, reward him with praise and a treat! For the first few weeks, don't just let him out. Go with him, so you can reassure him and reward him for going.

✱If you have children, don't let them crowd your dog, hug him, or squeal and run. Show them how to give the dog a treat with palm up and how to pet the dog on his chest or under his chin. They should wait for the dog to come to them, and have a treat ready when he does.

✱For the first week, mix the food you want to use with the food your dog was eating at the kennel, rescue, or breeder. Slowly, increase the amount of your food in the mixture.

✱During the first few days, leave your dog alone for a period of time, so he can get used to being alone. Train your dog to a crate by giving him treats and feeding him in the crate with the door open. Gradually, get him used to the door closed. Have chew toys in the crate for him.

✱On the first night, show your dog where you want him to sleep. Do not go to him if he barks. If you hear your dog fidgeting like he has to go to the bathroom or if you have a young puppy, take him to the bathroom at night without talking to him

✱Stay on a schedule for sleeping, feeding, and walking, so your dog can learn your routine and be housebroken more easily.

✱Expect accidents, even with a "housebroken" adult. In addition to learning your routine, an anxious dog may have loose bowel movements. Don't punish your dog. Clean the accident with an enzymatic cleaner and stay calm.

✱Ask for the behavior you want from the start. For example, when someone comes to the door, put your dog in a sit and reward him. Don't feed him from the table, and don't allow your children to do it either.

✱You can give an adult dog a new name. It may even be a good idea if he has been mistreated and associates his name with punishment. Say your dog's name often and when he looks at you, give him a treat.

✱Praise and reward your dog IMMEDIATELY for good behavior. This will encourage him to do it again. Try to anticipate and prevent unwanted behavior. For example, attach a leash to your dog before he goes in the family room for the first time, so you can prevent him from getting on the sofa.

✱Show your dog that you are a leader, so he can calm down and trust in you. Ask your dog to "SIT" before you put on his leash, feed him, or play with him. If your dog isn't trained to walk nicely on a leash, use a Gentle Leader, a Halti, or a no pull harness to keep him from pulling you down the street. Don't give your dog attention when he demands it. Call him over to you to give him attention after he has left you alone. Start obedience training with your dog.

✱Don't punish your dog. This won't help your relationship, and it won't make you a leader in your dog's eyes. What it might do is promote fearful aggression.

✱Take your dog to the veterinarian's office the first week, and bring his medical records. You may want to visit the office with your dog first, more than once if you can, and give him treats there to reduce his fear of going to the vet's.

✱Have close friends or relatives who spend a lot of time at your house come over during the first few weeks, so your dog gets used to them. Have them give your shy dog a treat to encourage him. Have them give your boisterous dog a treat to reward a calm greeting. You will need the latter on a leash, so you can help him with his behavior.

✱Expect at least a two-week "honeymoon", during which your dog will be more submissive to you, even if that is not normal to him. Once he feels that your home is his territory, his confidence will build and you will see his personality assert itself. During this time, work on issues. For example, reward him for good behavior around strangers.

✱If your dog was mistreated in his last home, it could take him months to gain confidence. Go at his pace, and reward him generously for small steps. Encourage him to go places. Never drag him.

✱Groom your dog every day, so he gets used to being handled. After a short grooming session, give him a treat, go for a walk, or play a game. If your dog is scared, brush only down his back and on his shoulders. For more dominant dogs, continue grooming until you are finished, even if this means you put him on a table or tie him. Give him treats as you are brushing.

✱ When you need to bathe your dog, put him on a mat in a dry tub, then add the water gradually after he is in the tub. This will be less scary for him.

Most of these ideas are from *Adopt the Perfect Dog: A Practical Guide to Choosing and Training an Adult Dog* by Gwen Bailey.

Resources

Recommended Websites:

✱www.petfinder.com—adoptable pets; shelters/rescues; resource library of dog-related articles

✱www.petsforlife.org—tip sheets on common puppy behavior, dog-training basics, and dog behavior issues

✱www.gooddogz.org—articles on choosing a dog, training, health, safety, and grooming; rescues

✱www.pets911.com—pre-adoption advice; health resources; shelters/rescues

✱www.populardogs.com —magazines on various breeds and on training and obedience (If you're considering a pit bull, *Training Secrets for Bully Breeds* is a must.)

✱www.dogwise.com—dog books that can be searched by topic

✱www.whole-dog-journal.com—natural care; alternative health care

✱www.srdogs.com—adoptable older dogs; rescues for older dogs; health advice

✱www.petloverscompanion.com—pet services and resources; shelters/rescues; articles (Washington, DC area)

✱www.metropets.org—pet services and resources; shelters/rescues (Washington, DC area)

Recommended Books

Before Choosing a Dog:

✱*Paws to Consider: Choosing the Right Dog for You and Your Family* by Brian Kilcommons and Sarah Wilson

✱*Mutts—America's Dogs: A Guide to Choosing, Loving, and Living With Our Most Popular Canine* by Brian Kilcommons and Michael Capuzzo

✱*Choosing and Caring for a Shelter Dog: A Complete Guide to Help You Rescue and Rehome A Dog** by Bob Christiansen

✱*Adopt the Perfect Dog: A Practical Guide to Choosing and Training an Adult Dog** by Gwen Bailey

*These two books also have good training and behavior advice!

Training:

✱ *The Power of Positive Dog Training* by Pat Miller

✱ *Don't Shoot the Dog: The New Art of Teaching and Training* by Karen Pryor

✱ *The Culture Clash* by Jean Donaldson

✱ *Way to Go! How to Housetrain a Dog of Any Age* by Patricia McConnell and Karen London

Behavior Issues:

✱ *The Toolbox for Remodeling Your Problem Dog* by Terry Ryan

✱ *Dogs Behaving Badly: An A-to-Z guide to Understanding and Curing Behavioral Problems in Dogs* by Dr. Nicholas Dodman

✱ *The Cautious Canine: How to Help Dogs Conquer Their Fears* by Patricia McConnell

✱ *Scaredy Dog: Understanding and Rehabilitating Your Reactive Dog* by Ali Brown

✱ *I'll Be Home Soon: How to Prevent and Treat Separation Anxiety* by Patricia McConnell

✱ *The Bark Stops Here* by Terry Ryan (for excessive barkers)

✱ *Mine! A Guide to Resource Guarding in Dogs* by Jean Donaldson

Body Language:

✱ *Canine Body Language: A Photographic Guide* by Brenda Aloff

✱ *The Other End of the Leash: Why We Do What We Do Around Dogs* by Patricia McConnell

✱ *What Your Dog is Trying to Tell You: A Head-To-Tail Guide to Your Dog's Symptoms - And Their Solutions* by John M. Simon, DVM

Exercise and Recreation:

✱ *Fitness Unleashed: A Dog and Owner's Guide to Losing Weight and Gaining Health Together* by Marty Becker, DVM and Robert Kushner, MD

✱ *Canine Adventures: Fun Thing to Do With Your Dog* by Cynthia D. Miller

✱ *The Dog Lover's Companion: The Inside Scoop on Where To Take Your Dog* (available at dogloverscompanion.com or from Avalon Travel)

✱ *Traveling with Your Pet: The AAA Pet Book* (lodgings and campgrounds rated by the American Automobile Association)

Debra Ekman is a dog trainer certified by Animal Behavior College and a member of the Association of Professional Dog Trainers. She has volunteered as an adoptions counselor with an all all-breeds rescue and as an adoptions counselor and trainer at two shelters. Debra founded **Your Dog's Friend**, a free service in Montgomery County, Maryland, that advises and educates dog owners before they choose their dog, after they bring home their new pet, or when they have questions about their dog's behavior. She lives with ten adopted dogs of her own.

To contact Debra about your dog, please call 301-983-5913 or contact her through Your Dog's Friend's website, www.yourdogsfriend.info.